MAJID DEHKORDI

The Best Interview Hacks

A Fast Easy Manual By A Career Coach In Japan

Copyright © 2024 by Majid Dehkordi

All rights reserved. No part of this publication may be reproduced, stored or transmitted in any form or by any means, electronic, mechanical, photocopying, recording, scanning, or otherwise without written permission from the publisher. It is illegal to copy this book, post it to a website, or distribute it by any other means without permission.

Majid Dehkordi asserts the moral right to be identified as the author of this work.

Majid Dehkordi has no responsibility for the persistence or accuracy of URLs for external or third-party Internet Websites referred to in this publication and does not guarantee that any content on such Websites is, or will remain, accurate or appropriate.

Designations used by companies to distinguish their products are often claimed as trademarks. All brand names and product names used in this book and on its cover are trade names, service marks, trademarks and registered trademarks of their respective owners. The publishers and the book are not associated with any product or vendor mentioned in this book. None of the companies referenced within the book have endorsed the book.

First edition

This book was professionally typeset on Reedsy.
Find out more at reedsy.com

It is hard to fail, but it is worse never to have tried to succeed.

Theodore Roosevelt

Contents

Acknowledgement	ii
Chapter 1: Introduction	1
Chapter 2: Pre-Interview Preparation	4
Chapter 3: During the Interview	14
Chapter 4: Post-Interview	22
Chapter 5: Conclusion - Seize Your Career Destiny	24
The 50 Most Common Industry Interview Questions	26
The 50 Most Common Academic Interview Questions	34
References	42
About the Author	45

Acknowledgement

A special thank you to Ms. Sunrise Eclipse, my editor and advisor, whose sharp insights and meticulous attention to detail have greatly enriched this manuscript. Her dedication and expertise have been instrumental in refining this work, ensuring that each page reflects clarity and precision. Her support has been invaluable throughout this journey.

I would like to thank my academic supervisor, Prof. Seiichiro Yonekura, whose guidance and wisdom have profoundly influenced my academic journey. Prof. Yonekura's relentless dedication to teaching and research has not only enriched my understanding but has also inspired me to pursue excellence in all my endeavors. His mentorship has been a beacon of knowledge and inspiration, and for that, I am eternally grateful.

I extend my heartfelt thanks to my work supervisor, Mr. Shah Haque, for his invaluable support and leadership. Mr. Haque's pragmatic approach to problem-solving and his unwavering support have significantly contributed to my professional growth. His mentorship has been crucial in helping me navigate the challenges of the industry, and his confidence in my abilities has empowered me to achieve my best.

Chapter 1: Introduction

Welcome to your game-changing career gadget! This book isn't just about getting by in job interviews - it's about owning them. Dr. Majid Dehkordi, a seasoned professional with over a decade of coaching in Japan's ultra-competitive market, has crafted this guide to turbocharge your interview skills. Whether you're a fresh graduate hitting the job scene, a professional eyeing a career jump, or a student targeting advanced degrees, this book is your blueprint for long-term success.

Dr. Majid Dehkordi, armed with a PhD in Marketing and Management and a career spent mastering Japan's demanding job market, breaks down his inspirational strategies into clear, actionable steps. Known for his innovative coaching techniques, Dr. Dehkordi's methods are not just theoretical; they're battle-tested tools designed to sharpen your skills and make you stand out. This book delivers his insights in a no-nonsense, practical format that will help you not just meet, but exceed the expectations of any interviewer, anywhere.

Do you think these strategies are only relevant for navigating Japan's tough job market? Think again! Dr. Dehkordi's techniques are universally powerful, ready to be deployed by anyone, anywhere. With this guide, no matter where you are in the world, you can elevate your interview game and beat out the competition. Get ready to transform your approach and take control of your career destiny with confidence and flair!

Why I suggest this book? Because the job market is an arena, and every interview is a performance that determines your future. Here you will learn not only how to prepare for an interview, but also how to execute successfully during the interview and how to follow up afterward effectively. This manual will equip you with a robust toolkit, actionable steps, and insider tips designed to elevate your interview skills beyond the competition.

From understanding what interviewers truly seek, to mastering the art of first impressions, to handling post-interview etiquette - this book covers it all. You'll get insights into:

- **Pre-Interview Preparations:** Tailoring your approach to different industries and positions.
- **During the Interview:** Techniques to remain composed and compelling under pressure.
- **Post-Interview Actions:** Strategies to leave a lasting impact and secure your position.

Moreover, we will dig into the 50 most common questions in both the industrial and academic interviews, giving you a comprehensive view of what to expect and how to respond with confidence.

In the past decade, the industry has seen rapid technological shifts, altering both business operations and the skills employers value. As a result, interview techniques have also evolved, requiring applicants to adapt to new methods like virtual interviews and behavioral assessments. Being up to date with these changes is crucial for job seekers aiming to meet modern employers' expectations.

Keep this in mind: a fulfilling job not only enhances your personal happiness and comfort but also positively impacts your family members. Being satisfied in your career can contribute to a longer, happier, and healthier life. Therefore, dedicating time and energy to master the skills

CHAPTER 1: INTRODUCTION

needed to secure your dream job is definitely worthwhile.

Let's embark on this journey together, and by the end of this book, you'll not just be ready for your next interview; you'll be poised to win it.

Chapter 2: Pre-Interview Preparation

Get ready to power up your interview preparation game! This chapter is all about setting the stage for a killer performance before you even step into the interview room. It's not just about avoiding rookie mistakes; it's about increasing your confidence to maximum levels and being so prepared that success is the only option.

A) <u>Learning about the Position</u>

Master the battlefield before you step foot on it! To truly stand out in your interview, you need to go beyond the basics and delve deep into understanding the company and the specific role you're applying for. Start your research by exploring the company's website. Dig into their products, discover their main competitors, and catch up on any recent news such as mergers, acquisitions, or expansions. Knowing the company's global scale and the CEO's vision can provide you with insights that make your responses more relevant and impactful.

Don't stop there, collect more information about your interviewers. Use platforms like LinkedIn to learn about their professional background. Knowing their current role, their career path, and their professional interests can help you connect more effectively during the interview. This knowledge not only shows your intelligence but also helps you tailor your answers to resonate with the interviewer's

CHAPTER 2: PRE-INTERVIEW PREPARATION

expectations and experiences.

For job-specific insights, thoroughly review the job description if available. It is your blueprint for the role's requirements and the company's expectations. Understand each listed responsibility and think about how your skills and experiences align with them.

For those applying to academic positions, a similar approach is required. Visit the university's website, explore the department you are applying to, and review the profiles of the interviewers. Academic interviewers often have detailed online profiles that include their research interests, publications, and teaching philosophy. Familiarizing yourself with these details can help you present yourself as a well-informed and compelling candidate who is genuinely interested in contributing to the academic community. By thoroughly researching both the company and the people within it, you equip yourself with the knowledge to ask insightful questions and give informed answers, significantly increasing your chances of making a memorable impression

B) Learning about Yourself

Step up and double-check your story! Before you shine in that interview, make sure you've mastered every single detail of your own resume. Begin by revisiting your resume in depth, Dive back into every job, project, research, and skill you've listed. Remember, interviewers will be tricky and they might throw a curve ball by asking about a project from way back. Be ready to come out on top by remembering all your wins, big or small.

Here's a real-life wake-up call: I had a client aiming for a top spot in academia who stumbled badly during his interview. When quizzed about a paper he published seven years prior, he blanked out and forgot the details. The interviewer replied back, "It's your own research, how can you not remember it?" This isn't just a minor hiccup; it's a major red flag to interviewers. It shows that you might not be as engaged or passionate about your career as you claim.

So, flip the script! Dive deep into your professional past and keep it fresh. And while you're at it, focus on your strengths and get real about your weaknesses. Own them, and more importantly, show how you're turning them around. This isn't just about avoiding mistakes; it's about showing confidence, competence, and growth. Show them that you're not just going through the motions, you're elevating your skills every day. This type of confident and self-aware presence will distinguish you in any interview.

C) Collecting Information and Using Different Tools

Ramp up your research efforts! In today's digital era, there's no reason not to be fully informed about the company or university you're looking to join. Hit up LinkedIn to learn about the company culture, key players, and any mutual connections who can offer insider insights. Don't just skim - dig deep. Wikipedia and the organization's own website are gold mines for understanding their history, major achievements, and future ambitions. This isn't casual browsing; it's strategic intelligence gathering.

But let's take it up a notch - connect with the real game-changers, the recruiters and HR professionals. These are the players on the inside track, and they often hold the keys to what goes down in the interview room. Reach out, build rapport, and don't shy away from asking them directly: What causes other candidates to stumble? What wins them over? This isn't just chitchat; it's gathering crucial intel that could help you avoid common pitfalls and propel you toward nailing that interview.

Remember, every piece of information is a potential edge in a competitive field. Use every tool at your disposal to arm yourself with

CHAPTER 2: PRE-INTERVIEW PREPARATION

knowledge. This is how you prepare to win, ensuring when you walk into that interview room, you're not just another candidate - you're the candidate they've been waiting for.

D) Confidence Booster

Power up, you're already in the door! Remember, if you've been invited to an interview, the company sees you as a potential asset. They've already checked out your resume and liked what they saw; now it's your turn to believe in that reflection. This is where your confidence must shine because it's your self-assurance and communication skills that will seal the deal.

Start by cataloging your strengths, specifically those that align directly with the job you're applying for. Write them down, say them out loud, and know them by heart. These aren't just skills; they're your arsenal. Next, turbocharge your confidence by tapping into the power of motivation. Explore the world of motivational speakers and industry gurus. Watch them, listen to them, and let their energy inspire you. Platforms like YouTube are bursting with inspirational content that can kick your confidence into high gear.

Meditation can also play a crucial role here. It's not just about calming your nerves; it's about centering your focus and sharpening your mind. A clear, focused mind projects confidence and controls the room. Combine this with the fire you've stoked from motivational speeches, and you'll walk into that interview not just thinking you can win it, but knowing you will. Each interview is a once-in-a-lifetime moment - own it and let your confidence be the key that turns the lock.

E) Mock Practice

How to boost your energy and step into the interview with confidence?

Practice makes perfect! To truly prep for the big day, you need to dive deep into mock interviews. Use the list of 50 common questions we've provided in Chapter 5 as your training manual. Go through each question, crafting and refining your answers. But here's where you turn up the heat: once you've practiced each question, circle back and answer it again with a fresh spin. Why? Because interviewers often rephrase and ask the same questions to test consistency and depth. You need to be sharp, versatile, and ready to handle curve balls.

Timing is key. Aim to keep your responses between 1 and 4 minutes. Too short, and you risk seeming underprepared or superficial, interviewers may think this applicant doesn't have enough information to add. Too long, and you might come off as talkative or unfocused. This isn't just about having answers - it's about delivering them with precision. For insights into the cultural differences and interview etiquette, reach out to those who've been there. Talk to people who've interviewed in the industry. Hit up recruiters or HR professionals - they've got firsthand experience of what works and what doesn't.

During your mock sessions, keep a critical eye on your performance. Time your answers, note any stumbling points, and relentlessly refine your delivery. For example, use a mirror, record yourself, or request a friend to play the interviewer. Each round is a chance to improve, to tighten your narrative, and to polish your presence. When you enter the actual interview, you won't just be responding to questions - you'll be mastering them.

Lastly, master the STAR method for engaging properly in behavioral interview questions. It stands for Situation, Task, Action, and Result. This technique isn't just about answering questions; it's about storytelling. Practice by explaining your past experiences in a structured way to manifest your problem-solving and critical thinking skills in real-world scenarios. Some may call it 'Success stories and accomplishments'. Here's a breakdown of each component, followed by multiple examples:

CHAPTER 2: PRE-INTERVIEW PREPARATION

STAR Components:

1. **Situation**: Describe a situation or scenario within which you performed a task or faced a challenge at work.
2. **Task**: Explain the actual task details or responsibility you had in that project/task.
3. **Action**: Describe the specific actions you took to handle the task or overcome the challenge.
4. **Result**: Share the outcomes or results of your actions. Highlight what you accomplished and what you learned through your actions.

Examples:

Example 1: About A Leadership Scenario: Can you describe a time when you led a team to achieve a goal? How did you achieve the goal?

Situation and Task: In my previous role as a project manager, I was leading a matrix project team, and our team was tasked with developing a new application with a tight deadline. My responsibility was to ensure the team stayed on track without delays and delivered the project on time without compromising quality. I had to make sure that the project's quality would satisfy the client.

Action and Result: I organized a kickoff meeting to define roles and set clear deadlines. I held daily stand-up meetings to monitor progress, addressed any roadblocks immediately, and provided regular updates to stakeholders. I also implemented a collaborative project management tool to improve communication. The team successfully delivered the feature two days ahead of schedule, resulting in positive feedback from the client and a 15% increase in customer satisfaction.

Example 2: About A Problem-Solving Scenario: Tell me about a time when you faced a significant technical problem at work and how you handled it.

Situation and Task: At my previous job, we encountered a major error with our database, causing significant downtime for our e-commerce platform. We also received some complaints from the Database users. I was responsible for identifying the root cause of the problem and fixing the error as quickly as possible to minimize revenue loss.

Action and Result: I quickly assembled a team of database experts and programmers and conducted a thorough analysis. We discovered a minor corruption issue in the data that could even lead to bigger problems in the future. I led the team in implementing a backup restore procedure, followed by a comprehensive data integrity check to ensure no further issues. We managed to restore the database within three hours, reducing the potential downtime from what could have been 12 hours or more. Our swift action saved the company an estimated $100,000 in potential losses and maintained customer trust. We also received positive feedback from our clients afterward.

Example 3: About A Conflict Resolution Scenario: Describe a time when you had to resolve a conflict between team members or handle an internal dispute.

Situation and Task: During a high-stakes client-facing project, two team members disagreed about the approach to a key technical component. As the team leader, it was my responsibility to mediate the conflict and ensure the project stayed on track. Especially this project was for a new client and we wanted to make a good first impression.

Action and Result: I scheduled a meeting with both team members to understand each of their perspectives. I facilitated open communication and encouraged a discussion to find common ground. We agreed on a hybrid approach that incorporated the best aspects of both ideas.

Both team members were also satisfied by this decision. The resolution improved team cohesion and allowed us to complete the project on time. The final product was praised by the client for its innovation, blending both team members' strengths.

Example 4: About A Time Management Scenario: Can you give an example of how you managed multiple priorities? How do you handle multitasking?

Situation and Task: As a marketing manager for a Pharmaceutical company, I was handling three major marketing campaigns simultaneously, each with tight deadlines. My task was to ensure all campaigns were executed effectively without any delays.

Action and Result: I created a detailed project plan for each campaign and prioritized tasks based on deadlines and importance. I used a well-known and user-friendly project management software to track progress and set aside specific times each day to focus on different campaigns. I also delegated some tasks to junior team members to balance the workload. All three campaigns were launched successfully within the deadlines. The campaigns collectively increased our client engagement by 20% and generated a significant uptick in leads. I also received positive encouragement feedback from my manager.

Some Tips for Using the STAR Technique:

- **Be Specific and Precise**: Provide concrete details rather than vague descriptions.
- **Be Concise and Right to the Point**: Keep your responses focused and avoid rambling.
- **Prepare in Advance**: Think of several success story examples before your interview.
- **Practice, Practice, and Practice**: Rehearse your success stories

to feel more confident during the interview.

Using the STAR technique effectively can help you articulate your experiences and skills clearly, making a strong impression on your interviewer.

F) Relationship with Headhunter or Hiring Company

Engage with your allies; headhunters and HR professionals are not just gatekeepers, they're your career accelerators! Understanding the crucial role these individuals play can dramatically elevate your job search game. Headhunters and HRs are in the trenches daily, pushing hard to match the right candidate with the right role. They know the ins and outs of the companies they recruit for, hold key insights into the hiring process, and genuinely root for your success - it reflects on their professional ability.

Think of your relationship with recruiters as a strategic partnership. They are your direct line to your dream job, often managing countless communications to champion your candidacy. You might not see it, but behind the scenes, they are diligently working towards your success. Their success hinges on yours, so transparency and cooperation are crucial. Be upfront about your skills, your aspirations, and even your reservations. This honesty not only fosters trust but also enables them to advocate effectively on your behalf.

Work closely with these professionals. Pay attention to their advice, respond promptly to their communications, and be flexible to their suggestions. Remember, when they reach out to you with opportunities or feedback, it's because they see a potential fit. Engage with them and value their efforts and feedback, they're the experts in the field, and their insights could be the component for your next big career move. Keep this relationship strong, respectful, and dynamic, and watch how

CHAPTER 2: PRE-INTERVIEW PREPARATION

it propels you closer to your goals.

G) Notes for Academic Applicants

Academic go-getters, listen up! The arena of academia demands not just smarts but strategy. Here's how you prepare to dominate those academic interviews, from Master's and PhD positions to professorships.

First off, stay sharp and updated on the research trends in your field. Knowledge isn't just power - it's your ticket to standing out. Show you're not just keeping up; you're pushing the boundaries and can bring fresh, innovative research ideas to the table.

Next, ignite your passion for both research and teaching. Higher academic roles demand a dual focus: you've got to be as passionate about delivering engaging lectures as you are about pioneering academic research. Demonstrate this enthusiasm clearly in your interviews. Show them that you're not just there to contribute but to inspire.

Building a solid relationship with your potential academic supervisor starts from that very first interview. Show you're a standout listener, eager for guidance, and keen to collaborate. This isn't about mere agreement - it's about showing you value their expertise and are ready to grow under their mentorship. Academic professors value a challenging mindset over simply agreeing with everything - they prefer thinkers, not just yes-men.

Prepare a killer research and teaching statement. This is your manifesto, your vision for your role in academia. It's your chance to articulate not only what you plan to research but how you'll convey these complex ideas to students. Make it compelling, clear, and visionary. Get these strategies down, and you're not just going for the job - you're going for the respect and recognition that sets the foundation for a flourishing academic career. Let them see that you're not just another applicant; you represent a bright future for academia.

Chapter 3: During the Interview

Alright industry champions, you've made it to the big day. This is where the rubber meets the road. Everything you've done up to this point has set the stage for this moment. Now, it's Show Time. Let's explore how to absolutely crush your interview with the precision and power that will leave your hiring manager in admiration.

A) Arrival at the Interview Location

Get There Early: First things first, arrive early. I'm not talking about on time; I'm talking about early. If your interview is at 10 AM, you better be there by 9:30 AM. Arriving early for your interview is crucial; aim for at least 15-30 minutes ahead of time. This demonstrates your commitment and reliability. Sometimes, finding the office can be tricky. One of my clients missed her interview because she couldn't locate the building on time. If you rely on public transportation, anticipate weather and delays from trains, buses, and traffic. Build in extra time to avoid stress. Early arrival lets you settle your nerves, review your notes, and mentally prepare, displaying your seriousness and dependability.

Dress to Dominate: Your appearance matters. Dress like you're already the CEO. For men, a sharp suit, polished shoes, and a confident tie. If the company allows casual clothing, wear your best clothes. For women, a professional suit or dress that shows authority. Remember, how you dress is a reflection of how you feel about yourself. Look powerful, feel powerful, be powerful.

Behavior: From the moment you step into the building, you're being evaluated. Be polite to everyone, from the receptionist to HRs and Hiring Managers. You never know who might have a say in the hiring process. Smile, maintain eye contact, and carry yourself with confidence. You're not just applying for a job; you're demonstrating why they can't afford to lose you.

B) Online Interview Setup

Tools and Applications: For those doing online interviews, your setup speaks professionalism. Ensure you have a professional background – no messy rooms or distracting elements. Invest in good lighting, a quality webcam, and a reliable microphone. Test your devices beforehand to avoid any glitches. When it comes to online interviews, your virtual stage is just as important as if you were meeting in person. First, ensure your applications are also solid. Install and test any necessary applications like Teams, Skype, Zoom, or Meet in advance. This is a common pitfall; out of every 10 interviews, at least one gets canceled or rescheduled due to avoidable technical issues. Don't let this be you. Companies always blame the candidate, not the technology; because it's up to you to be prepared. Ensure your internet connection is stable, your camera and microphone are working, and your background is professional. At least you can use virtual background filters, which are available in most applications.

Body Language and Presence: Even online, body language matters. Sit up straight, lean slightly forward to show engagement, and maintain eye contact through the camera. Your presence needs to be felt even through the screen. Dress professionally from head to toe – and no pajama pants. You never know if you'll need to stand up!

C) Introducing Yourself and Motives

The Perfect Pitch: Alright, listen up! Your self-introduction is your elevator pitch. Master it. Keep it concise, confident, and compelling. Highlight who you are, what you bring to the table, and why you're excited about this opportunity.

When you're introducing yourself in an interview, you need to nail the perfect pitch. This is not the time to talk about your personal hobbies or private life - companies don't care about your weekend plans. Keep it concise and professional - focused on your education, work experience, and accomplishments related to the job.

Here's how you do it: Start with your education. Mention the university you attended and what you studied. Then, move on to your work experience. List the companies you've worked for and the positions you've held. Highlight key accomplishments and how you've developed your skills over time.

Think of it as a timeline: "I graduated from XYZ University with a degree in ABC. I started my career at Company 1 as a Junior Analyst, where I improved XYZ processes. Then, I moved to Company 2 as a Senior Analyst, leading a small team to achieve ABC results. Currently, I'm with Company 3 as a Project Manager, where I've successfully implemented DEF strategies."

Keep it tight, no more than 4-5 minutes, unless they ask for more details. And make sure your introduction isn't less than 1 minute - too short can make you seem unprepared. This shows you're professional, prepared, and focused on what matters to the company. Remember,

CHAPTER 3: DURING THE INTERVIEW

this is your shot to impress - make every second count.

D) Technical Questions and Impressing the Hiring Manager

Showcase Your Skills: When it comes to technical questions, preparation is a crucial key. Study the job description and align your skills with what they're looking for. Use the STAR method (Situation, Task, Action, Result) to structure your answers.

Go the Extra Mile: Impressing the hiring manager isn't just about answering questions; it's about showing initiative. Bring a portfolio of your previous work or explain them, propose new ideas, or demonstrate how you've solved similar problems in the past.

Here's where you really shine. When it comes to technical questions, this is your moment to go beyond the basics. Exceptionally, it's fine to talk longer than 4 minutes here - this is your chance to showcase your skills, so take the time you need.

First off, explain your success stories. If you have experiences directly related to the job you're applying for, lay them out. Talk about the challenges you faced, the actions you took, and the results you achieved. Be specific and detailed - this isn't the time for vague generalities. If you don't have direct experience related to this job, don't sweat it. Use success stories from other roles and explain how you applied similar methods that could lead to success in this new position.

Here's the kicker: Highlight your strengths. Talk about your leadership capabilities, your hard work, your excellent communication skills, your ability to work in a team, your time management skills, and your strong scientific background. Don't just say you have these strengths - prove it with examples.

For instance, if you're great at time management, talk about a project where you had to manage multiple deadlines and how you delivered on time. If you're a strong leader, discuss 2 or 3 specific situations where you led a team to achieve significant results.

Now, let's talk about impressing the hiring manager. Making a strong bond with the hiring manager, or your professor in the case of academic positions, is crucial. Companies typically interview multiple applicants for each position. Based on my experience, big companies interview 10- 15 applicants and proceed with 2- 3 candidates to the final stage for comparison. Sometimes, hiring managers view all job applicants indistinguishably, much like background characters in a movie whose presence fades from memory as soon as their scene ends.

So, it's important to leave a lasting impression. Pay close attention to what the hiring manager says during the interview. Find anything you could have in common, such as graduating from the same university, studying the same course, having the same degree, resolving work issues in a similar manner, or agreeing with their suggestions and opinions. If there's nothing in common, at least admire their achievements.

Before you leave that interview, you must make sure the hiring manager knows you are very interested in the position. This is crucial. Most applicants leave without expressing their enthusiasm, and that's a big mistake. Look the hiring manager in the eye, tell them you are genuinely excited about the opportunity, and clearly state you want the job and are eager to proceed to the next step. Make your interest known - this could be the difference between getting an offer and being forgotten.

Remember, this part of the interview is all about demonstrating that you're not just a good fit for the job - you're the best fit. Show them how your background, your skills, and your successes align perfectly with what they're looking for. Make them see that hiring you is the best decision they could make.

E) HR and Personality Assessment

CHAPTER 3: DURING THE INTERVIEW

Alright, listen up! HR and personality tests are designed to see if you're a good fit for the company culture. Be honest, but also be strategic. Understand what the company values and align your answers to reflect those values. Practice common personality tests online to get comfortable with the format.

When you get to the HR and personality assessment, you're in a different game. HRs are out to measure who you are beyond your resume. They want to know if you're going to be a team player or a problem magnet. They're checking if you can fit into their organizational structure - whether it's a small, large, fast-paced startup or a slow-moving corporation. They'll dig into your background, looking for any red flags like a history of crime or harassment.

Now, when it comes to company culture, you've got to show you can adapt. If they're looking for someone who thrives in a fast-paced, high-pressure environment, be honest. Can you handle it? If not, it's better to bow out gracefully now than to crash and burn later.

HR will also ask about your salary expectations, location preferences, and your start date. Here's the deal with salary: If you've got a recruiter, let them do the negotiating. Recruiters know the company's budget, they know how to play the game, and they can get you the best deal. If you're flying solo, tread carefully. You want to get what you're worth without scaring them off with sky-high unrealistic demands. The best move? Share your current salary and ask them to make a competitive offer that reflects your value. And remember, for academic positions, salaries are usually fixed and non-negotiable.

Bottom line: HR wants to make sure you're not just qualified on paper but that you'll also mix well with the team and the company culture. Show them you can fit in, adapt, and thrive in their environment, and you'll be one step closer to landing that job.

F) Additional Tips and Hacks

Ask Insightful Questions: When it's your turn to ask questions, go beyond the basics. Ask about the company's vision, their competitors, challenges they're facing, and how you can contribute to overcoming those challenges. This shows you're thinking long-term and are genuinely interested in the company's success.

For academic interviews, it's crucial to ask about the future of the position. What are the long-term opportunities? Is there a pathway to a permanent role or tenure-track assignments? Find out what's expected of you by the end of the contract and what milestones you should aim for. Show them you're not just thinking about getting in the door - you're planning to stay and make a significant impact.

And here's an advanced tip: make sure to ask about opportunities for further professional development. For example, ask your supervisor if they plan to hire you as a Research Assistant or Post-Doctoral fellow after your project ends. This shows you're committed to growth and continuous improvement, traits every employer values.

Remember, asking insightful questions doesn't just give you valuable information - it demonstrates your genuine interest in the role and your proactive mindset. It tells the hiring manager you're serious about this opportunity and ready to take on the challenges ahead. So, get ready, jump in, and ask standout questions that will differentiate you from others.

G) Additional Presentations/Notes for Academic Applicants

Prepare to Present: If you're an academic applicant, be ready to give a presentation. This is your time to shine. Structure your presentation clearly, practice it multiple times, and anticipate questions. Use visuals to enhance your points, but don't rely on them. Your knowledge and passion should be the star of the show.

Detailed Notes: Bring detailed notes and be ready to discuss your research, publications, and teaching philosophy. Show how your work aligns with the institution's goals and how you can contribute to their mission. Be prepared to engage in deep discussions about your field and demonstrate your expertise.

Chapter 4: Post-Interview

Alright, you've dominated the interview, left a lasting impression, and now you're feeling good. But listen up - the game isn't over yet. What you do after the interview can make or break your chances. This short chapter is all about the power moves and strategies you need to make once you walk out that door. Buckle up, because we're diving into the crucial post-interview strategies.

A) <u>Follow Ups</u>

First things first: the follow-up. This is where you show them you're serious, committed, and still at the top of your game. Within 24 hours of your interview, Send a personalized thank-you email to everyone you met. Keep it short, sweet, and powerful. Remind them of a key point from your conversation, reiterate your enthusiasm for the position, and make sure they remember your name. You're not just another candidate - you're the candidate.

And don't stop there. If you haven't heard back within a week, follow up again. Be persistent, but not annoying. Show them you're still interested and eager to hear their decision. This is a delicate balance, but if you nail it, you'll stand out as someone who's genuinely motivated and proactive.

For those working with recruiters, communication is crucial after the interview. Send positive and motivational feedback to your recruiter about the interview and some details you discussed. Recruiters use this information to impress the company about you. Your feedback helps them pitch you better, showing the company that you're the perfect fit.

B) Decision Making

Now, let's talk about decision-making a little. You're not just waiting around for them to choose you - you're evaluating them too. When you get an offer, it's time to weigh your options. Does this position align with your career goals? Will it challenge you and help you grow? Look beyond the salary. Consider the company culture, the team you'll be working with, and the long-term opportunities.

If your family plays a role in the decision, discuss the offer and its potential with them. I recommend making a decision before you are presented with an offer. Typically, once companies extend an official offer letter, they give a limited deadline for decision-making (usually one week). Therefore, it is better to make a potential decision step by step during the process, especially before the actual offer is presented.

Chapter 5: Conclusion - Seize Your Career Destiny

As we wrap up this inspirational journey through the art of acing job interviews, let's engrave these truths not just in our minds but in our actions. Dr. Majid Dehkordi's insights have armed you with more than just strategies; they've rebooted your mindset, transforming you from a hopeful candidate into a commanding job market contender.

You've been equipped with the tools to not only tackle but dominate interviews across any industry or academic field. From pre-interview preparations that fine-tune your approach to mastering the interview room dynamics and nailing post-interview tactics, every chapter has been a building block toward your ultimate success.

Remember, the job market is your battleground, and every interview is a performance that could launch your career to new heights. The techniques detailed here are your secret weapons - use them to showcase your strengths, articulate your ambitions, and demonstrate your readiness to contribute meaningfully to potential employers.

Now, think about the change in perspective you've experienced. You started this book looking for tips; you're finishing it as a strategist. Dr. Dehkordi's foolproof methods aren't just about getting a job - they're about winning the career of your dreams.

So, what's next? It's time to step out with the confidence of a seasoned professional. Approach every interview as if it's the defining moment of your career. Whether you're a fresh grad or a professional pivoting to a new challenge, the world is now your stage. Go out there, armed with knowledge, strategy, and unshakable confidence, and take control of your career destiny.

Never settle, never stop, and remember - every interview is an opportunity to demonstrate that you are not just a candidate; you're the candidate they need. Make it count. Let's make those job offers rain down as you choose your path, equipped with the ultimate manual to turning interviews into gateways for your career growth.

Get ready, get out there, and own your future. You're not just ready for your next interview; you're ready to conquer it.

If this book fired up your interview game, please post a positive review on Amazon or wherever you got your copy. Your feedback is powerful - it helps others find this book and secure their dream jobs!

The 50 Most Common Industry Interview Questions

Here are the top 18 knockout questions you're going to face in just about every interview. We've laid out killer strategies and slick answers for each, so you're locked and loaded. And don't sweat it - there are more practice questions to help you gear up and throw down your best answers! Get ready to dominate!

- **Tell me about yourself. Introduce yourself.**

"I am an experienced professional with over ten years of experience in the tech industry, focusing on project management and software development. I hold a Master's degree in Information Technology Management from the University of ABC. Throughout my career, I have progressed from an IT Analyst to a Senior Analyst at my first company, gaining a promotion in just three years. Subsequently, I joined my second company as a Senior Analyst and was promoted to Manager within two years, where I have successfully led diverse teams to integrate user-centric designs, significantly enhancing product functionality and user experience."

[**Note**: Avoid discussing personal life and family matters during the interview]

- **Why are you looking for a new job?**

"While I've greatly appreciated the opportunities at my current company, I'm looking for new challenges that align more closely with my expertise in innovative tech solutions. I'm particularly interested in a role that allows me to leverage my skills in a larger, more dynamic environment to drive impactful changes."

[**Note**: While sometimes people search for a new job due to industrial reorganizations, internal conflicts, sexual and power harassment, and mass firings in global firms, please focus on the positive aspects of your motivation]

- **Why are you interested in working for us?**

"I am deeply impressed by your company's commitment to innovation and quality, which resonates strongly with my professional ethos and skills. Your recent initiatives in sustainable technology particularly caught my attention, aligning perfectly with my background in sustainable systems. Having thoroughly researched your company's developments and achievements through your website, I am convinced that now is the ideal time for me to join your team and contribute actively to your ongoing and future projects"

[**Note**: Do not go to an interview unprepared; you need to check the company's website and learn about its products and services]

- **What do you want to do in our company?**

"I am interested in the Project Senior Manager role, where I can bring my expertise in team leadership and project execution to not only meet but exceed project milestones. My proactive management style and ability to anticipate project needs are qualities that I believe will significantly benefit your team."

- **Why don't you apply internally for a promotion in your current company?**

"While there have been opportunities for advancement, the specific challenges and learning opportunities your company offers, especially in international project management, are more in line with my career aspirations."

[**Note**: Do not mention that you have applied internally for a promotion, but your internal application was rejected. Sometimes hiring managers think if their own company has rejected them, then why should we hire them?]

- **How do you deal with problems and difficult colleagues?**

"I approach workplace challenges with a focus on open communication and empathy. For instance, I once led a project where differing opinions led to tension. By facilitating a mediation session where everyone shared their views, we found a compromise that respected all opinions and enhanced project outcomes."

- **Tell us about your experience on Project A/Product B.**

"In Project A, I spearheaded a team that developed a mobile application, which improved customer engagement by 30% within six months of launch. My role involved overseeing the project life cycle from conception through to deployment, ensuring all technical requirements were met."

[**Note**: Do not forget to review your resume before the interview, since interviewers will ask you questions about past projects that you might have already forgotten about]

- **Tell us about your strengths and weaknesses.**

"My key strength is my ability to see projects through from inception to completion, ensuring all objectives are met. A weakness I continue to work on is my tendency to take on too much myself. I've been learning to delegate more effectively to enhance team capacity and efficiency."

[**Note**: For weaknesses, please make sure that your weakness is not a deal breaker, but rather a weakness that you have already fixed and turned into a strength]

- **Where do you see yourself in 5 years?**

"In five years, I see myself in a leadership role within your company, driving key projects and mentoring the next generation of project managers. My goal is to not only advance my own skills but also contribute to the company's long-term success."

- **Tell us your opinion about your current company's Product or Management.**

"My current company is great at fostering a culture of innovation. However, I believe there can be improvements in how projects are scoped and scheduled. I've seen firsthand how a more strategic approach can drive efficiency, something I'm eager to bring to your team."

- **How is your relationship with your current boss, colleagues, or subordinates?**

"I have built strong, respectful relationships in all directions at my current job. My boss has been a great mentor, and I've developed a collaborative approach with my colleagues and subordinates, fostering a team-oriented environment."

[**Note**: Even if you do not like your manager/company/colleagues, do not bad mouth them in the interview]

- <u>How do you want to develop relationships in our company in the future?</u>

"I aim to build robust professional relationships based on mutual respect, trust, and collaboration. I plan to actively engage in team meetings, seek feedback, and contribute positively to our shared goals, ensuring a cohesive team dynamic."

- <u>Tell me about an accomplishment you are most proud of.</u>

"One of my greatest achievements was leading the turnaround of a lagging software development project, bringing it back on schedule and reducing costs by 20%. This success was due to my strategic realignment of resources and rigorous schedule management."

- <u>What are your salary requirements?</u> <u>When can you start in our company?</u>

"I'm looking for a salary that reflects the responsibilities of the role and my experience, which I believe is in line with your company's current pay structure for this position. I am able to start with a standard notice period of four weeks, ensuring a smooth transition from my current role."

[**Note**: Do not give them an unrealistic salary expectation. Please study your industry's salary standards and smoothly negotiate your value]

- **How much do you know about us? Who are our competitors?**

"I am well- aware of your company's leadership in the market and your main competitors, including X and Y. I admire how your company differentiates itself through a strong focus on both innovation and customer satisfaction, which are critical areas I have direct experience in."

- **How do you handle a situation where you don't know the answer or solution?**

"I believe in being honest about my knowledge gaps and actively seeking out information through research or consultation with knowledgeable peers. My approach is to be proactive in learning and adapting, ensuring that I can find or develop effective solutions."

- **What new skills and programs have you learned in your previous jobs?**

"Recently, I completed an advanced course in Agile Project Management, which has significantly enhanced my project planning and execution skills. Additionally, I've learned to use advanced features of Project Management software which have increased my efficiency."

- **What questions do you have for me?**

"I'd love to know more about how the company supports professional development and learning. Additionally, I'm interested in how the company measures success for this role specifically over the first 12 months."

[**Note**: Even if you asked many questions during the interview, make sure that you ask at least one or two questions at the end of the interview]

The following 32 questions are for you to practice with your answers. These are still important depending on the situation.

1. Why was there a gap in your employment?
2. How would you overcome a disagreement with your manager? Tell me about a time when you disagreed with your boss.
3. How do you manage work overload?
4. What are three things your former manager would like you to improve on?
5. Are you willing to relocate or travel?
6. Tell me about a time you made a mistake. What was your biggest failure?
7. How did you hear about this position?
8. What would you look to accomplish in the first 30 days/60 days/90 days on the job?
9. Tell me how you handled a difficult situation in the past. Tell me about a challenge or conflict you've faced at work, and how you dealt with it.
10. What motivates you?
11. How do you handle pressure, and stress?
12. What would your direct reports say about you? If I called your boss right now and asked him what is an area that you could improve on, what would he say?
13. What were your bosses' strengths/weaknesses?
14. Are you a leader or a follower?
15. What makes you uncomfortable? What's your greatest fear?

16. What are some of your leadership experiences? What's your management style? (For leadership roles)
17. How would you fire someone? (For leadership roles)
18. What do you like the most and least about working in this industry?
19. Would you work 40+ hours a week? How do you manage work-life balance?
20. What other companies are you interviewing with?
21. What are you looking for in a new position? What are the challenges of this position?
22. How do you handle failure? And How do you handle success?
23. Can you explain why you changed career paths in the past? Please tell us why you changed jobs from company A to B in the past.
24. How do you like to be managed?
25. What did you like most about your last position? What did you like least about your last position?
26. How do you evaluate success?
27. Describe a time when you had to use your presentation skills to influence someone's opinion.
28. Explain a time when you had to be persuasive in getting your ideas across.
29. Tell me about a time you had to gather information from multiple sources. How did you determine which information was relevant?
30. How do you ensure clear communication with team members who are not familiar with your area of expertise?
31. What measures do you take to protect company data and adhere to privacy laws?
32. Can you describe a situation where you had to take a leadership role unexpectedly? How did you handle it? Describe a time when you had to adapt quickly to a significant change at work.

The 50 Most Common Academic Interview Questions

Here are the top 17 questions you need to conquer any academic interview; these are the ones you're most likely to face every time. We've laid out not just the questions but also killer guidelines and example answers to help you crush it. For the rest? We've got those listed too, so you can hammer out your answers and get in the game- shape. Practice makes perfect, and this is where you start.

- **Can you elaborate on your experience with Research Topic ABC?**

"I have been deeply involved with Research Topic ABC for over five years, focusing on its implications in sustainable development. My engagement has been both theoretical and applied, involving extensive fieldwork and collaboration with interdisciplinary teams to advance practical applications of our findings."

- **What strategies do you use for developing new research proposals?**

"My approach to developing new research proposals involves a thorough literature review to identify gaps, collaboration with peers for diverse insights, and aligning the objectives with ongoing or emerging scientific questions and funding priorities."

- **What is innovative about your research?**

"My research introduces novel computational models that significantly reduce the complexity of analyzing big data in environmental studies, setting it apart from conventional methods. This innovation not only enhances accuracy but also increases efficiency, offering clear advantages over existing approaches."

[**Note**: Don't exaggerate about your research projects. Show the importance of your research without undermining others' work or overstating your contributions.]

- **How is the relationship with your current Academic supervisor/Colleagues?**

"I maintain a highly productive and respectful relationship with my academic supervisor and colleagues. We have a collaborative working environment where constructive feedback and support are pivotal, fostering personal and professional growth."

[**Note**: Don't speak ill of your academic supervisors or colleagues. Even if your ideologies differ, they are respected members of the research community]

- **What do you consider to be your most significant research accomplishments?**

"My most significant accomplishment is the development of a model that predicts ecological impacts of urban development with high accuracy, which was published in 'Journal X.' This work has been pivotal in shaping policy in urban planning."

- **How do you bridge the gap from research to research users/industry?**

"I actively engage with industry stakeholders during the research process to ensure the applicability of our findings. By integrating their feedback and focusing on scale-able solutions, we ensure that our research has practical and immediate applications in real-world settings."

- **How do you plan to manage your research project day-to-day?**

"I employ a structured approach using time and project management tools to track progress, set deadlines, and allocate resources efficiently. Regular meetings with all team members ensure that we remain on target and address any issues promptly."

- **Describe your teaching experience. What is your teaching philosophy?**

"I have taught undergraduate and postgraduate levels, focusing on interactive learning. My philosophy is centered on fostering critical thinking and application of knowledge, encouraging students to explore real-world implications of theoretical concepts."

- **Have you supervised Doctoral/Master candidates?**

"Yes, I have supervised three doctoral candidates and several master's students. I find the experience enriching as it sharpens my mentoring skills and strengthens my ability to guide young researchers through complex research challenges."

- **How do you ensure student engagement in large and small lectures?**

"In large lectures, I use multimedia presentations and real-time polls to maintain engagement. For smaller groups, interactive discussions and problem-solving sessions help keep students actively involved."

- **What have you done to improve your knowledge?**

"I continuously seek to improve my expertise through advanced courses, and workshops and by staying updated with the latest research in my field. Engaging with new technologies and methodologies is also a key part of my professional development."

- **What do you expect from your future Academic supervisor?**

"I look for mentorship that challenges me and provides opportunities for growth, alongside support in navigating the complexities of academic research and career advancement."

[**Note**: Academic supervisors prefer candidates who can collaborate closely yet are capable of conducting research independently when necessary. Maintain a balance between reliance and independence]

- **What challenges are you expecting if you join us?**

"Transitioning into a new research environment will be challenging but exciting. I anticipate adapting to new institutional dynamics and integrating into your existing research teams, which I am fully prepared to handle with enthusiasm and commitment."

- **What kind of Statistical tools or IT Applications have you**

used in your research projects?

"I have used a range of tools including R, Python for statistical analysis, and MATLAB. Additionally, I am proficient in using SQL and advanced Excel for data manipulation and visualization."

[**Note**: Do not limit yourself to only the tools you currently know. If there are other tools you are unfamiliar with, demonstrate a passion for learning and using them]

- **How do you ensure the integrity and accuracy of your research data?**

"I adhere strictly to ethical research practices, conduct regular audits of our data collection and analysis processes, and use robust statistical methods to ensure validity and reliability of our data."

- **Describe your experience with peer-reviewed publications. How do you handle feedback?**

"I have published extensively in peer-reviewed journals. I view feedback as a crucial element of personal and project improvement and integrate constructive criticism to refine my work."

- **What role do conferences and seminars play in your professional development?**

"Conferences and seminars are vital for networking, staying updated with the latest research developments, and sharing our work with the global academic community. I have presented at multiple international conferences, which has significantly enriched my perspective and research approach."

THE 50 MOST COMMON ACADEMIC INTERVIEW QUESTIONS

The following 33 questions are for you to practice with your answers. These are still important depending on the situation.

1. How do you decide what gets top priority when scheduling your time?
2. How do you integrate new technologies or methodologies in your teaching and research?
3. What techniques do you use to motivate researchers?
4. Are there specific funds or grants you are considering applying for?
5. What impact has your research had in your field?
6. What do you see yourself doing in 5 or 10 years time?
7. Who are the key researchers in your area? How does your work compare with that of the key researchers?
8. How does your work align with current trends or funding priorities?
9. Who has influenced you the most in your academic career?
10. How do you handle conflict within your research group?
11. Have you undergone formal training in higher education teaching? How do you accommodate diverse learning styles in your classroom?
12. What aspects of your teaching would you like to improve?
13. If there is an opportunity, how do you feel about transferring your research into innovation or spin-outs?
14. Describe a research problem you faced and what you learned from it.
15. How do you balance your time if multiple challenges arise simultaneously?
16. What experience do you have in attracting funding? How can you assure us you will be able to secure larger amounts of funding? Where will you apply for grants, and what are your backup plans

if unsuccessful?
17. How do you keep your course content and materials up-to-date with current trends in the field?
18. What techniques do you use to keep yourself organized?
19. If you had to choose one, would you consider yourself a big-picture person or a detail-oriented person? Why?
20. Who was your favorite Professor/Researcher and why?
21. Tell me about a time when you had to give feedback to a sensitive colleague.
22. How do you motivate yourself and your team?
23. Describe a time when you had to advocate for a public change in a process or policy.
24. Tell me about a time when you saw a problem and took the initiative to correct it rather than waiting for someone else to do it.
25. Describe a time when you were not only responsible for leading a team but also had to perform some of the team's tasks.
26. How do you handle situations where you need to juggle multiple projects/clients at the same time?
27. Please explain your Master's thesis/Doctoral thesis and your most recent research project.
28. Tell me about a time when you worked under close supervision or extremely loose supervision.
29. How do you measure success in your job?
30. Describe a time when you had to make a difficult professional decision. What do you find are the most difficult decisions to make?
31. How have you handled working with someone who doesn't like you? What do you do if you disagree with a team member?
32. What steps do you take to form positive, productive working relationships with new colleagues?

33. Can you give an example of how you have contributed to improving the curriculum in your previous roles?

References

Throughout the book's creation, we pulled insights from a variety of corners; think articles, books, and several websites. Consider these resources as our sidekicks, providing the backup needed to pack this guide with powerful content without directly quoting them. They were in the ring with us, making sure every piece of advice hits just right!

1. M Dehkordi, S Yonekura, F Hesami, (2013) Face-to-face communication versus computer-mediated communication: A media evolution model. International Journal of Multimedia, 2 (1).

   https://bioinfopublication.org/viewhtml.php?artid=BIA0002102

1. RL Gordon, (1998) Basic Interviewing Skills. Waveland Press.

   https://books.google.com.tr/books?id=LfoVAAAAQBAJ&printsec=frontcover&hl=tr#v=onepage&q&f=false

1. Kathryn L. Cottingham, (2017) *Interviewing for an academic job.* Guarini School of Graduate and Advanced Studies.

   https://graduate.dartmouth.edu/student-support/career-services/int

REFERENCES

erview-practice-techniques/interviewing-academic-job

1. Doyle, A. (2020). "Top Job Interview Tips for College Students." The Balance.

https://www.thebalancemoney.com/top-job-interview-tips-for-college-students-2059837

1. Bhosale, U., & Bhosale, U. (2021, July 15). 10 common academic job interview mistakes to avoid. *Enago Academy*.

https://www.enago.com/academy/academic-job-interview-mistakes-to-avoid/

1. Trull, S. G. (2024). *Strategies of Effective Interviewing*. Harvard Business Review.

https://hbr.org/1964/01/strategies-of-effective-interviewing

1. Indeed Editorial Team (2022). 21 Interview Techniques To Increase Opportunity To Be Hired.

https://www.indeed.com/career-advice/interviewing/best-interview-technique

1. Johnston, L. (2023). *Top ten tips for preparing for academic interviews*. career-advice.jobs.ac.uk.

https://career-advice.jobs.ac.uk/jobseeking-and-interview-tips/top-ten-tips-for-preparing-for-academic-interviews/

1. Emerick J. (2023). *20 common university interview questions and expert tips for answers.* Oxford Summer School 2024 | Oxford Scholastica Academy.

https://www.oxfordscholastica.com/blog/20-common-university-interview-questions-and-expert-tips-for-answers/

1. *Prepare for an academic interview.* (2024). The University of Edinburgh.

https://careers.ed.ac.uk/students/postgraduates/phd-students/make-it-happen/prepare-for-an-academic-interview

1. *Oliver, V (2005), 301 smart answers to tough interview questions: Free Download, Borrow, and Streaming:* Naperville, Ill. Sourcebooks.

https://archive.org/details/301smartanswerst0000oliv_n5m6

About the Author

Dr. Majid A. Dehkordi stands at the forefront of the recruitment and human resources industry as the Senior Director at Starlight Group in Tokyo and the Regional Head of Recruitment at Logical Choice Ltd. With a distinguished career specializing in HR, recruitment, and managerial consulting across the Asia-Pacific market, Dr. Dehkordi has become a pivotal figure in shaping the careers of thousands of professionals. His expert coaching has guided many through the complexities of industrial and academic job searches, helping them rise to become leaders and innovators in their respective fields.

Holding a PhD in Marketing and Management from the prestigious Hitotsubashi University, Dr. Dehkordi's academic pursuits and professional expertise span a broad array of interests, including Human Resource Management (HRM), Communication Studies, Entrepreneurship, and Green Technologies. His research has contributed significantly to the understanding of contemporary market dynamics and the development of effective human capital strategies in today's fast-evolving corporate landscape.

Dr. Dehkordi's commitment to fostering talent and innovation goes beyond mere business acumen; it is a passion fueled by the belief that every professional has the potential to impact their industry profoundly. He empowers his clients to seize that potential, not just to succeed but to transform their environments. As you turn the pages of this book, you are invited to harness his insights and strategies, refining your approach to the challenges of job interviews and career advancement.

Let his journey inspire you to carve your path to success, armed with knowledge, confidence, and the drive to achieve greatness.

www.ingramcontent.com/pod-product-compliance
Lightning Source LLC
Chambersburg PA
CBHW072002210526
45479CB00003B/1034